CREATIVE VENTURES
Mysteries & UFO's

Written by Rebecca Stark
Illustrated by Karen Birchak

The purchase of this book entitles the individual teacher to reproduce copies of the student pages for use in his or her classroom exclusively. The reproduction of any part of the work for an entire school or school system or for commercial use is prohibited.

ISBN 978-1-56644-574-0

© 2016 Barbara M. Peller

Educational Books 'n' Bingo

Previously published by Educational Impressions, Inc.

Printed in the U.S.A.

Table of Contents

TO THE TEACHER 4
WILLIAMS' MODEL 5

First Impressions 6
The Abominable Snowcreature 7
Bigfoot 8
Was That for Real? 9
What a Trap! 10
Don't Fence Me In! 11
Nessie 12
Urquhart Castle 13
Point of View 14
Keep Loch Ness Clean 15
Big Bird 16
Double Trouble 17
Special Report: Creature Sighted 18
The Lines of Nazca 19
Mysterious Places 20
Atlantis: the Lost Island 21
The Mayans 22
The Codices of the Mayans 23
Travel Agency: We Specialize 24
It Pays to Advertise 25
Flight 19 26
A Ghost Ship 27
Joshua Slocum 28
Roanoke: the Lost Colony 29
A Ghostly Vacation 30
Dear Mr. Holmes: 31
"It's Elementary" 32
What Happened Here? 33

Surprise Ending 34
Edgar Allan Poe 35
That's a Puzzlement! 36
The Lindberg Kidnapping 37
Private Eye 38
Here's My Card 39
Wanted: Private Eyes 40
Observations 41
A Basketful of Clues 42
Conundrums 43
Mysteries of the Mind 44
Mystery of the Sky 45
Math Alias 46
UFO's 47
Close Encounters of the First Kind 48
Close Encounters of the Second Kind 49
Close Encounters of the Third Kind 50
Alien Anthropologist 51
Strange Spectator 52
30 Tons of *What*? 53
There's So Much to Ask! 54
What's the Question? 55
What Can You Make of These? 56
UFO Sounds 57
An "Alien's" Point of View 58
Earthly Artifacts 59
An Eventful Drive 60
War of the Worlds 61
Flying Saucers 62

FOLLOW-UP ACTIVITIES 63-64

To the Teacher

The open-ended activities in this book were designed to extend the imagination and creativity of your students and to encourage students to examine their feelings and values. Specifically, they focus upon the cognitive and affective pupil behaviors described in Williams' Model: fluent thinking, flexible thinking, original thinking, elaborative thinking, risk-taking, complexity, curiosity and imagination. (See the summary of Williams' Model on page 5.)

Students must learn to recognize problems and to produce and consider a variety of alternate solutions to those problems. Teachers, therefore, should urge students to defer judgment of their ideas until they have produced many alternatives. They should also encourage them to let their imaginations run wild so that their ideas include clever, unusual alternatives as well as the more obvious ones.

Each volume of the **CREATIVE VENTURES SERIES** centers around a different area; however, the area is broad and the nature of the activities is interdisciplinary.

I hope you and your students enjoy your ventures into creativity!

Rebecca Stark

A SUMMARY OF WILLIAMS' MODEL

COGNITIVE-INTELLECTIVE

Fluent thinking— to generate a great number of relevant responses.

Flexible thinking— to take different approaches in order to generate different categories of thought.

Original thinking— to think in novel or unique ways in order to produce unusual responses and clever ideas.

Elaborative thinking— to add on to, or embellish upon, an idea.

AFFECTIVE-FEELING

Risk-taking— to have courage to expose yourself to failure or criticism and to defend your ideas.

Complexity— to be challenged to seek alternatives and to delve into intricate problems or ideas.

Curiosity— to be inquisitive and to be willing to follow hunches just to see what will happen.

Imagination— to feel intuitively and to reach beyond sensual or real boundaries.

First Impressions

According to prevalent scientific opinion, 2-legged human-like beasts cannot exist; however, many responsible people believe them to be real. The beasts these men and women have reportedly seen vary from pygmy to giant; they also vary in their degrees of beastliness (for example, the amount of hair covering their bodies).

Suppose you have just met someone for the first time. The individual tells you that he/she saw an 8-foot, 2-legged, human-like creature that was completely covered with black hair except for portions of its face. Describe your first impressions of the individual.

What questions will you ask the individual to determine whether he/she is telling the truth (or at least believes he/she is telling the truth)?

1.

2.

3.

4.

5.

What questions will you ask the individual to find out if he/she has had a hallucination?

1.

2.

3.

4.

5.

© 1987 Educational Impressions, Inc.

The Abominable Snowcreature

Yeti and abominable snowcreature are two of the names given to the human-like beasts believed by many to inhabit the snows of the high Himalayas of south central Asia. Evidence of their existence, however, is circumstantial, and most scientists doubt that they really exist.

Yetis have been described as ranging from 5½ to 6½ feet (1.7 to 2 meters) tall. Reddish-brown to black hair is said to cover their entire bodies except for their faces.

Abominable means detestable or loathsome. List the things you would describe as abominable.

1.
2.
3.
4.
5.

A young yeti is very upset. He has just overheard a human refer to him as abominable. Suggest some things that his mother might say to comfort him.

1.
2.
3.
4.
5.

© 1987 Educational Impressions, Inc.

Bigfoot

Sasquatch, or Bigfoot, is the name given to the human-like beasts allegedly seen in the northwestern part of the United States and in the Canadian province of British Columbia. These 2-legged creatures are described as 7 to 8 feet (2.1 to 2.4 meters) tall with broad shoulders and deep chests. Tracks that have been found have been 16 to 22 inches (.4 to .6 meters) long. They are described as having human-like arms and legs and ape-like faces. Like the yetis of the Himalayas, they are also said to be covered with hair except for their faces.

Suppose you were hiking through the woods with a friend and saw a sasquatch. Write the adjectives that would describe how you would feel.

1.

2.

3.

4.

5.

List all the possible ways you might react.

1.

2.

3.

4.

5.

Put a ✓ next to the idea you think you would choose.

© 1987 Educational Impressions, Inc.

Was That for Real?

Many people believe that the sasquatches and yetis are really bears. They say that bears sometimes go over their tracks as they walk, thereby making the tracks appear larger than they really are.

Take the point of view of a person who does not believe in the existence of creatures such as sasquatches and yetis. List all the reasons you can think of to support such a view.

Now write an entry in your diary as the same person who has just seen such a creature!

Dear Diary,

Today I saw...

What a Trap!

Design a trap to capture Bigfoot.

What qualities must your trap have?   List the possible things to do with Bigfoot once you capture him/her.

Put a ✓ next to those things you consider unethical.

Put a ★ next to the idea you think you would choose.

Draw a picture of your trap.

Explain how it works:

_____
_____
_____
_____
_____
_____
_____
_____

Don't Fence Me In!

Imagine that you are Bigfoot. You have been captured by a human. Write a soliloquy describing how you feel.

(A soliloquy is a literary or dramatic speech in which a character talks to himself or reveals his thoughts in the form of a monologue without addressing a listener.)

Nessie

Loch Ness is a lake in Scotland, near Inverness. Except for the peat that runs into it from the rivers, it is basically unpolluted. (Peat is moss or other vegetable matter that is partly decayed; it is dark brown.) The peat, however, makes the water almost opaque. It is in these murky waters that many people claim to have seen a huge prehistoric-type creature with one or more humps. That creature is affectionately called Nessie.

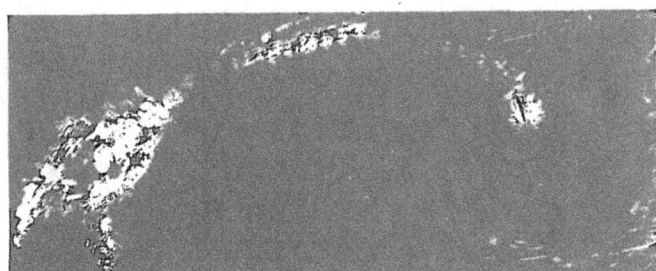

In the 1970's scientists set up sonar and underwater photographic equipment. With the use of computer enhancement, some of these photos showed what appeared to be a huge, diamond-shaped fin, a flippered body and a long, bending neck. Some naturalists concluded that this was positive proof of Nessie's existence, but scientists remain divided in their opinions.

What questions would you like to ask nearby residents?

_____
_____
_____
_____
_____

What would you like to ask scientists involved in the study?

_____
_____
_____
_____
_____

Urquhart Castle

Many of the reported sightings of Nessie have been made from Urquhart Castle. Create an ad for the travel section of your newspaper to entice tourists to stay in Urquhart Castle.

TRAVEL SECTION   T–1

Point of View

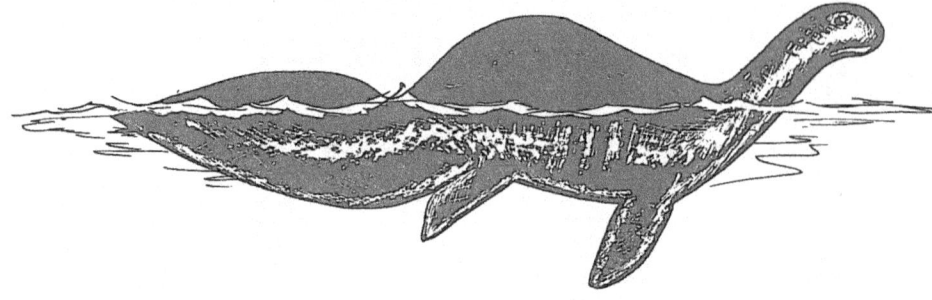

Write your feelings and views of the Loch Ness monster from three different points of view:

No. 1: An owner of a nearby souvenir shop

_____
_____
_____
_____

No. 2: A tourist convinced it is all a hoax

_____
_____
_____
_____

No. 3: An 8-year-old child who has just arrived at Loch Ness and has just been told of Nessie for the first time

_____
_____
_____
_____

© 1987 Educational Impressions, Inc.

Keep Loch Ness Clean!

You have been put in charge of a committee to keep Loch Ness and the surrounding area clean. Create three posters to encourage visitors to keep the area clean. Be original!

Big Bird

Fossilized pterosaur bones had been previously found in the area. These bones were over 60,000,000 years old. They had a wingspread of 51 feet. Many people believed that the big bird seen in 1976 was a survivor of this ancient species.

In 1976 many reliable witnesses reported the sighting in Texas of a huge bird that resembled the prehistoric pterosaur. State wildlife officials tried to find the creature, but after a few months gave up the search.

Create a conversation between the first person to report the sighting of the creature and the police officer who took the call.

Witness: _____

_____

_____

_____

Police Officer: _____

_____

_____

_____

© 1987 Educational Impressions, Inc.

Double Trouble

Combine two unusual creatures or monsters about which you have heard or read in order to form a new creature.

Creature No. 1: _____

Attributes, or qualities:

Creature No. 2: _____

Attributes, or qualities:

Put a ✓ next to those qualities of Creature No. 1 and Creature No. 2 that you want your new creature to possess.

Describe your new creature.

Draw a picture of your new creature.

List some possible names for your new creature.

Write the name you like best above your picture.

Special Report: Creature Sighted

Write a believable report for a local newspaper describing the sighting of the creature you described in the previous activity.

The Lines of Nazca

If you were to fly high above the vast pampas (nearly treeless grasslands) near Nazca, Peru, you would see a series of straight, intersecting lines alternating with huge drawings of animals. Among the drawings are a 150-foot monkey and a 600-foot hummingbird! They were drawn by the people of the ancient Nazca civilization in pre-Incan times.

Hypothesize, or guess, the reasons these lines might have been drawn. Think of as many possible reasons as you can.

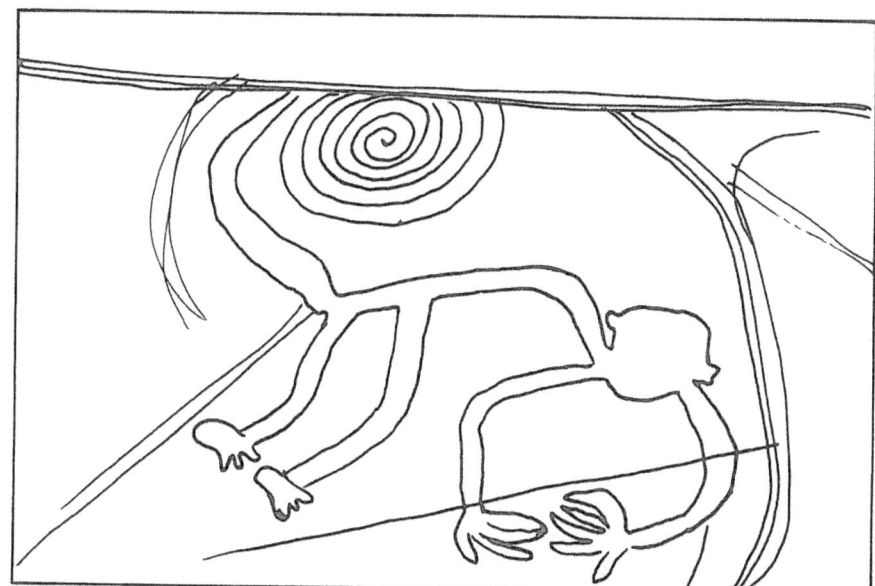

Mysterious Places

There is a place near Santa Cruz, California, where nature does not seem to follow her rules! Balls roll up hill! Trees grow in a manner resembling corkscrews! Compasses go crazy! No one is sure why these unusual gravitational properties exist. Some scientists believe a large meteorite might be buried beneath the mountain.

Propose some different theories to explain the strange occurrences. Don't be afraid to be outlandish!

Create your own Mystery Place.

Where is it? _____

What's unusual about it? _____
_____
_____

Think of possible names.

Put a ✓ next to the one you like the best.

Draw a picture that shows why your spot is so unusual.

Atlantis: the Lost Island

Atlantis is a legendary island continent which, according to ancient tradition was located in the Atlantic Ocean, west of the Pillars of Hercules. According to Plato, the paradise island sank beneath the sea during an earthquake. Some people are convinced that Atlantis really existed; however, no real proof of its existence has ever been found.

Ancient tradition tells us that Atlantis was a paradise — a place of beauty and delight. List the things and conditions you would expect to find in a paradise.

Draw a picture of your paradise.

The Mayans

The Mayan civilization of southern Mexico and Central America flourished from the Third Century to the Sixteenth Century when the Spaniards arrived. Archaeologists have learned that every twenty years (even more often in the larger cities) the Mayans abandoned their pyramids, palaces and other monuments and set up new ones. Then suddenly, all the the building stopped. Tikal, the largest Mayan city, had its last monument erected in A.D. 869.

Hypothesize as to why the Mayans abandoned their sites every twenty years and rebuilt their monuments elsewhere.

Hypothesize as to the reasons their civilization ended.

© 1987 Educational Impressions, Inc.

The Codices of the Mayans

The Mayans, like several other early Indian societies of Central and South America, wrote records of their history in books called codices. Each codex contained brightly colored picture writing. These codices would have provided a great deal of information about the Mayan civilization if the Spanish priests hadn't destroyed most of them. Because of their destruction, much of the Mayan civilization still remains a mystery to us!

Write two letters in which you express your opinion of the destruction of the codices from two different points of view: as an archaeologist studying the Mayans and as one of the priests who destroyed the artifacts.

ARCHAEOLOGIST

Dear _____ ,

Sincerely,

PRIEST

Dear _____ ,

Sincerely,

Travel Agency: We Specialize!

You own a travel agency that specializes in mysterious places — places where unusual things happen or have been seen.

Think of as many names as you can for your new agency.

Now design a logo, or symbol, for your company. Sketch your ideas in the boxes. Put a ✓ next to the one you like best.

It Pays to Advertise

Create some slogans and/or jingles to help you advertise your travel agency. Use the name you liked best from the last activity.

Use the logo you liked best in the last activity and the slogan or jingle you like best in this activity to create an ad for the yellow pages of your phone book.

© 1987 Educational Impressions, Inc.

Flight 19

There have been many disappearances of ships and aircraft within a small, concentrated area known as the Bermuda Triangle. Over 100 planes and ships — with more than 1,000 persons aboard — have been lost at sea, never to be found.

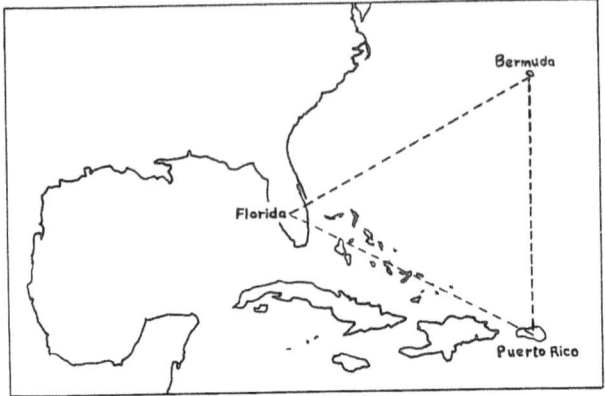

One of the mysteries involved Flight 19 of the U.S. Air Force. On December 5, 1945, 5 Avenger bombers took off on a routine training flight known as Flight 19. They left from Florida and headed into the area now known as the Bermuda Triangle. They were never seen again. Lt. Taylor called the control tower at 3:45 P.M. He reported that they were lost and that the compasses didn't work. At 4:00 the tower heard Taylor hand over command to Captain Stiver. Stiver, too, reported that they were flying aimlessly. As hard as they tried, the people in the tower could not get a message to Flight 19. The last words that came through from Flight 19 were: "It looks like we are...." One of the search planes that was sent to look for the Avengers was also lost and never again seen.

Complete the message in ways that might explain what happened. Include all of your ideas, no matter how far-fetched!

"It looks like we are _____

_____

_____."

"It looks like we are _____

_____

_____."

"It looks like we are _____

_____

_____."

© 1987 Educational Impressions, Inc.

A Ghost Ship

One of the strangest disappearances in the Bermuda Triangle happened as early as 1881. It involved the sighting of a beautiful schooner as it drifted near the *Ellen Austin*, commanded by Captain Baker. The schooner was found to be in excellent condition. It had a full supply of food and water. In fact, except for the people aboard, all that was missing was the log book and name plank. Captain Baker left part of his crew on board the "ghost" ship and the two ships headed for Boston. For two days nothing strange happened. Then a storm set in and the two ships lost contact. When the crew of the *Ellen Austin* found the schooner, the crew was not on it. The food hadn't been eaten and the beds didn't appear to have been slept in. The new log book was gone! Once again Baker convinced some of his crew to board the ill-fated ship. This time the ship disappeared in a mist. When the mist cleared a few seconds later, the schooner was gone. It was never found again!

Hypothesize as to what happened. Try to think of many possibilities.

Create a list of questions you would ask Captain Baker if you had a chance to interview him.

© 1987 Educational Impressions, Inc.

Joshua Slocum

Another incident of the Bermuda Triangle involved a world-renowned sailor, Joshua Slocum. In 1895 Joshua Slocum, at the age of 51, became the first known person to sail around the world alone! He accomplished this outstanding feat in his 37-foot, poorly equipped boat, the *Spray*. His 46,000 mile journey took three years to complete. This great sailor, however, was destined to become a casualty of the Bermuda Triangle. In 1909, after stopping for supplies in Miami, he set out to sea on a one-man journey to the West Indies. Joshua Slocum was never seen nor heard from again!

List the adjectives that would describe a person who would make a journey around the world in a small boat alone.

Imagine that you are Joshua Slocum. Write an entry in your diary as if written near the completion of your journey around the world. Describe how your feelings have changed since you first set out on your journey.

Roanoke: the Lost Colony

In 1585 Sir Walter Raleigh sailed to the New World with a band of colonists. The colonists were supposed to settle on Roanoke Island, but they got sidetracked in their search for gold and the settlement failed. In 1587 Raleigh brought another group of settlers to Roanoke; however, the supplies he sent the next year never reached them. When Raleigh returned in 1590, not a person was there. There was no sign of violence. On a tree was carved the word Croatan, the name of a friendly Indian tribe on the coast. Perhaps that was a clue — perhaps not!

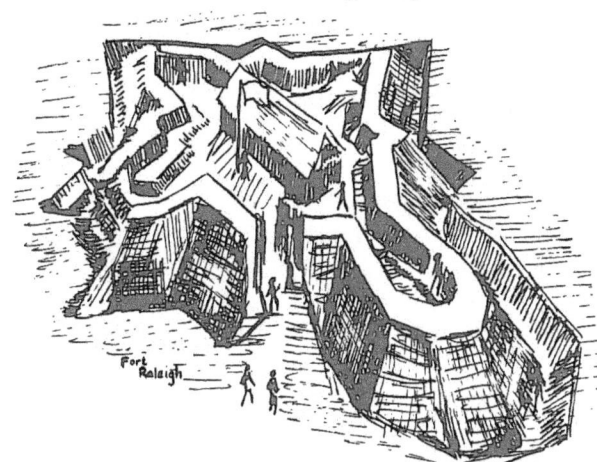

Hypothesize as to what might have happened to the colonists. Include all of your ideas, no matter how far-fetched!

Would you have made a good pioneer?

My Traits That Would Make Me a Good Pioneer

My Traits That Would Make Me a Poor Pioneer

© 1987 Educational Impressions, Inc.

A Ghostly Vacation

There is a book entitled **The Ghostly Register**, written by Arthur Myers and published by Contemporary Books, Chicago, Illinois. Each chapter focuses upon a different location in the United States where ghosts reportedly have been seen or heard.

Would you want to spend your vacation at one of the places described in **The Ghostly Register**?

_____
_____
_____
_____
_____
_____
_____
_____
_____

Think of some alternate names for the book.

_____
_____
_____
_____
_____
_____
_____
_____
_____

© 1987 Educational Impressions, Inc.

Dear Mr. Holmes...

Sir Arthur Conan Doyle was an English author who lived from 1859 to 1930. His tales of Sherlock Holmes were so popular that some people came to believe that the fictional detective really existed! Every once in a while letters arrive at 221B Baker Street in London requesting the aid of Mr. Holmes in unraveling a mystery.

Write a letter to Sherlock Holmes from someone requesting his assistance in solving a case. Summarize the details of the mystery in your letter.

Mr. Sherlock Holmes
221B Baker Street
London, England

Dear Mr. Holmes:

Sincerely,

"It's Elementary"

The famous fictional detective Sherlock Holmes often preceded the explanation of his logic to his associate, Dr. Watson, with the expression, "Elementary, my dear Watson."

Think of as many words and phrases as you can that have a similar meaning as "elementary."

How many words can you make by using the letters in the word "elementary"? Try to think of at least 25!

E-L-E-M-E-N-T-A-R-Y

What Happened Here?

Imagine you are a detective who has just come across the following scenes. Hypothesize and try to guess what might have happened to lead to each of the situations. Be creative and try to think of several unusual ideas!

What Happened?

_____
_____
_____
_____
_____
_____
_____

What Happened?

_____
_____
_____
_____
_____
_____
_____

© 1987 Educational Impressions, Inc.

Surprise Ending

Think of a mystery story you have read in a book or seen on television or in the movies.

Summarize the plot.

How did it end?

Now write a new ending to the story.

Edgar Allan Poe

Edgar Allan Poe was born in Boston, Massachusetts, in 1809. He is considered to be the creator of the American Gothic tale, detective fiction and even science fiction. (Gothic is the term used to describe a style of fiction that stresses the grotesque, mysterious and desolate.)

With the "Murders in the Rue Morgue" Poe is said to have created a new form of literature — the detective story! In it he created the character C. Auguste Dupin. Dupin solves the mysteries by methodical and logical reasoning.

The murders in the "Murders of the Rue Morgue" were carried out by an orangutan. Create 3 mystery plots in which the villain (or at least the villain's accomplice) is an animal.

Plot #1	Plot #2	Plot #3

That's a Puzzlement!

★Mystery is described in the dictionary as something that is not fully understood or that baffles or eludes the understanding.

List all the people, places, events, etc. which are mysterious to you.

★The American Heritage Dictionary, Second College Edition

The Lindberg Kidnapping

One of the most publicized cases of all time involved the kidnapping of the baby of Charles and Anne Lindberg on March 1, 1932. Charles Lindberg was known throughout the world. Five years earlier he had become the first to fly across the Atlantic Ocean. He was thought of as a hero and the world mourned when the baby was finally found dead close to their home. Bruno Hauptmann was later found guilty of the murder. Many believe others were involved, but they were never caught. The truth died with Mr. Hauptmann when he was put to death on April 3, 1936.

Pretend that you have been kidnapped by illiterate kidnappers. You even have to write your own ransom note! Be original! Write 1 to your family, 1 to a friend and 1 to your teacher trying to convince them to pay the ransom.

Dear _____ ,

Dear _____ ,

Dear _____ ,

© 1987 Educational Impressions, Inc.

Private Eye

You want to open a detective agency. The first thing you must do is to think of a name. Be creative and think of as many original names for a detective agency as you can.

Put a ✓ next to the name you like best.

Here's My Card

You now must make up a business card for your new agency.

First, design some possible logos to use on your card and stationary.

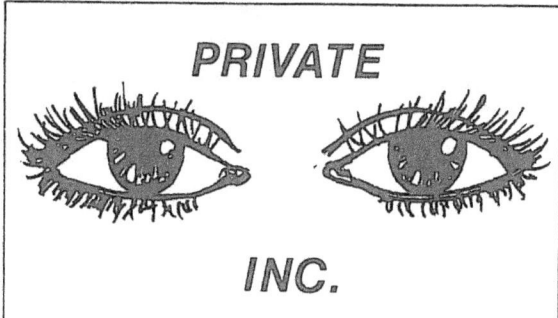

Now use the logo you like best to create a business card. Try a few different layouts.

© 1987 Educational Impressions, Inc.

Wanted: Private Eyes

Your detective agency is doing so well that you must hire more detectives! What qualities do you think a good detective should have.

1.   6.

2.   7.

3.   8.

4.   9.

5.   10.

Keeping in mind the above qualities, write a help wanted ad to attract the kind of person you'd like on your staff.

**CLASSIFIED
HELP WANTED SECTION**

Observations

Detectives must be very observant, for seemingly unimportant details often prove to be relevant clues. How observant are you?

Observe the things you see, smell or hear inside the room and out the window. Apply what you observe to other things. For example, the design you notice on a book cover might make an interesting pattern for the wallpaper in your bedroom. List all of your ideas.

1.

2.

3.

4.

5.

6.

7.

8.

9.

10.

Draw a picture to illustrate one of your ideas.

A Basketful of Clues

An anonymous tipster has left a basketful of clues at the doorstep of your detective agency. Also in the basket is a note begging you to solve the case. Unfortunately, you do not know to which case the note refers!

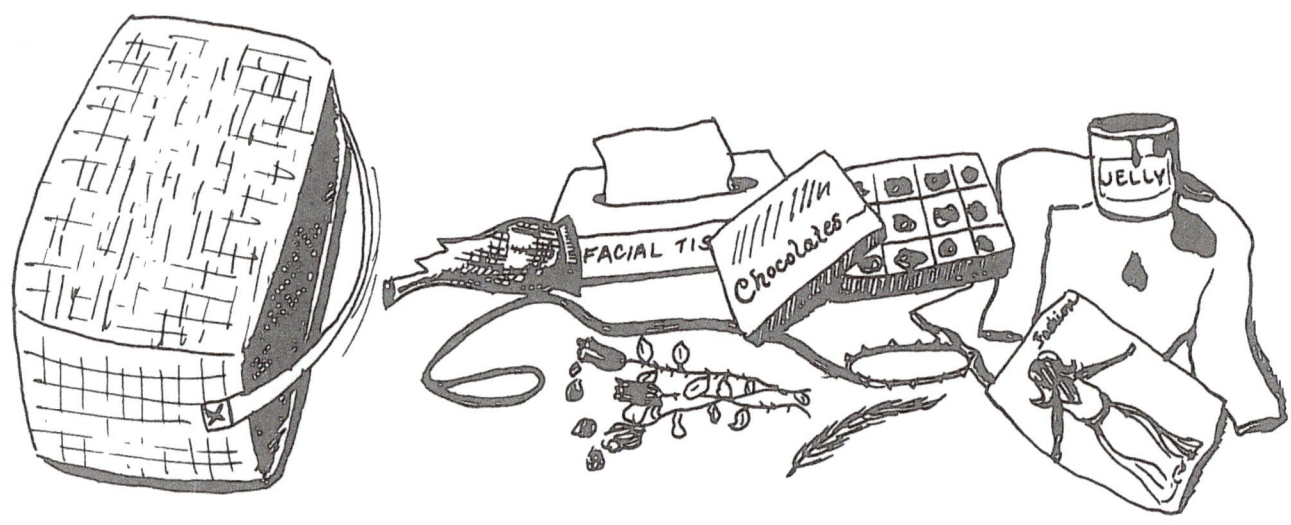

Use the clues in the basket to hypothesize, or guess, possible crimes. Summarize what might have happened for each idea.

1.

2.

3.

4.

5.

Now choose the idea you like best and embellish it with details to make an interesting mystery.

_____
_____
_____
_____
_____

Conundrums

A conundrum is a very perplexing question. It often refers to a riddle whose answer is a pun or to a problem whose solution is purely speculative.

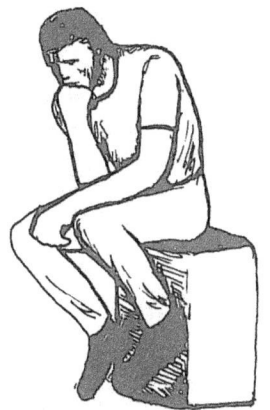

What are some other names we give to things of a perplexing nature?

1.
2.
3.
4.
5.
6.
7.
8.
9.
10.

Hypothesize as to the possible stories behind these headlines. Be creative and try to think of several ideas for each. They don't have to be true!

*Vice-President Calls
President's Announcement
a Conundrum!*

*Teachers Say
School Board's Decision
Is a Conundrum!*

Mysteries of the Mind

ESP is an acronym. It stands for **e**xtrasensory **p**erception. That means that it is perception outside the normal range of the senses: hearing, sight, smell, touch and taste. Another term for the power to perceive things that are out of the natural range of human senses is clairvoyance.

Suppose you were clairvoyant and had the ability to see or know about things that are not normally perceived by our senses. What could you do to take advantage of your clairvoyance?

Use the box on the right to advertise a business that you could start in which you would somehow use your special ability.

Mystery of the Sky

Things that we understand today were frightening and mysterious to the ancients. Today, for example, we know that a solar eclipse occurs when the moon is directly between Earth and the sun. When the moon is near enough to Earth so that its apparent size is greater than the apparent size of the sun, the lunar disk hides the solar disk.

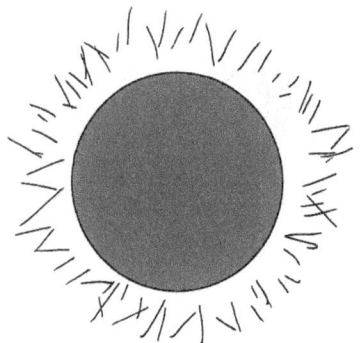

When things are farther away, they look smaller. In other words, their apparent size becomes smaller than their true size. Draw a picture that illustrates apparent size.

Write an account of a total solar eclipse from the point of view of an ancient.

_____
_____
_____
_____
_____
_____
_____
_____
_____
_____
_____

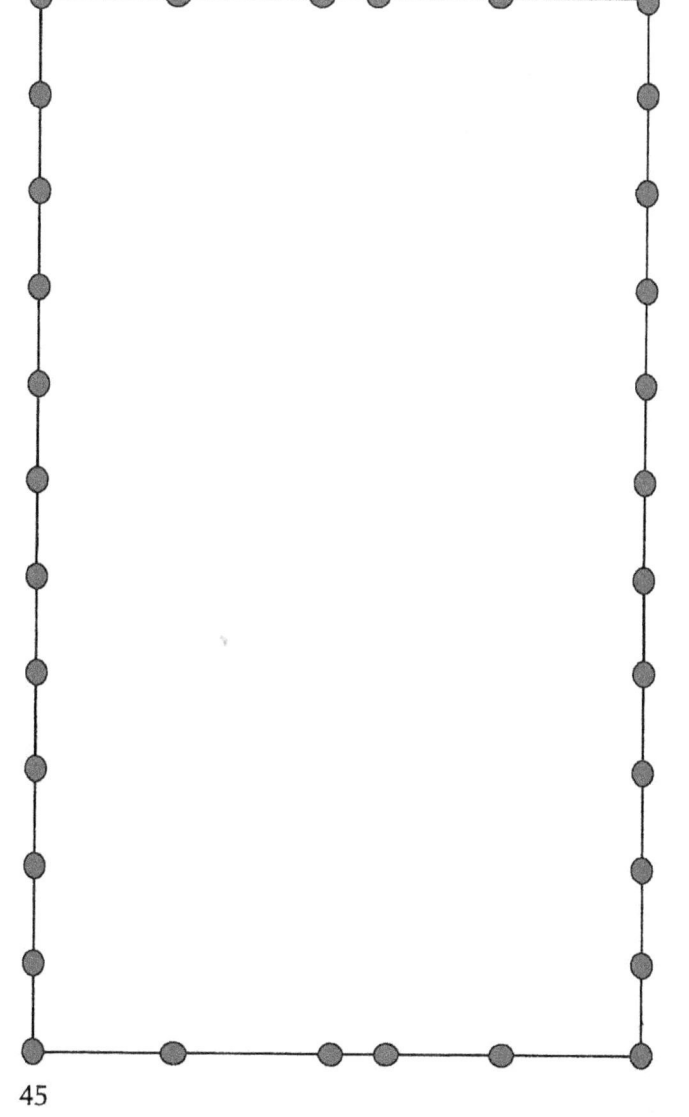

© 1987 Educational Impressions, Inc.

Math Aliases

An alias is an assumed name. As an adverb "alias" means otherwise named: "Jones, alias Smith," for example. Many criminals have aliases so that they aren't easily identified. We might also say that numbers have aliases, for they, too, have different names which mean the same quantities. For each of these numbers, list as many "aliases," or other names, as you can.

"Be on the lookout for 10, alias 5 × 2, alias 9 + 1, alias 20 ÷ 2..."

18　　　　　**36**　　　　　**20**

UFO's

The term UFO, or unidentified flying object, refers to any sighting the observer does not understand. Most UFO sightings have later been identified with astronomical and meteorological phenomena such as bright planets, meteors, auroras and ion clouds, and terrestrial phenomena such as aircraft, birds, searchlights and balloons. Some people believe that those that remain unidentified are spaceships from other parts of the universe.

UFO is an acronym. An acronym is a word formed from the initial letters of the main words in a name. List all the acronyms you can think of. Then make up different names for which those acronyms might stand.

For example:

NASA— National Aeronautics and Space Association

NASA— National Association of Super-Ants

Think of other names for which the acronym UFO might stand.

Close Encounters of the First Kind

Dr. J. Allen Hynek, scientific director for the Center for UFO Studies, classified UFO sightings as follows:

Close Encounters of the First Kind: Someone sights a UFO but has no connection with it.

Close Encounters of the Second Kind: The UFO leaves behind some physical evidence or acts upon people or our environment.

Close Encounters of the Third Kind: A lifelike being is seen in or near the UFO.

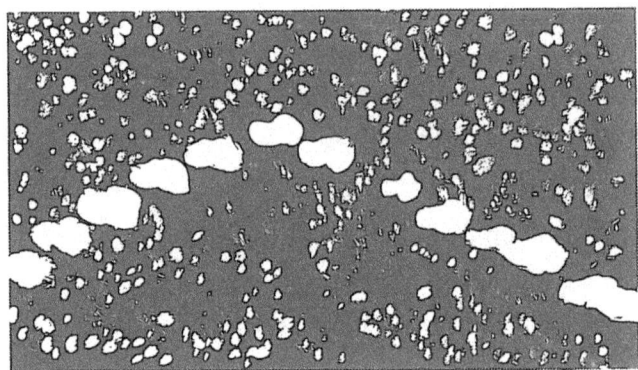

List all the things that might be mistaken for a UFO.

Close Encounters of the Second Kind

Close encounters of the second kind are those in which the UFO leaves behind some physical evidence or acts upon people or our environment.

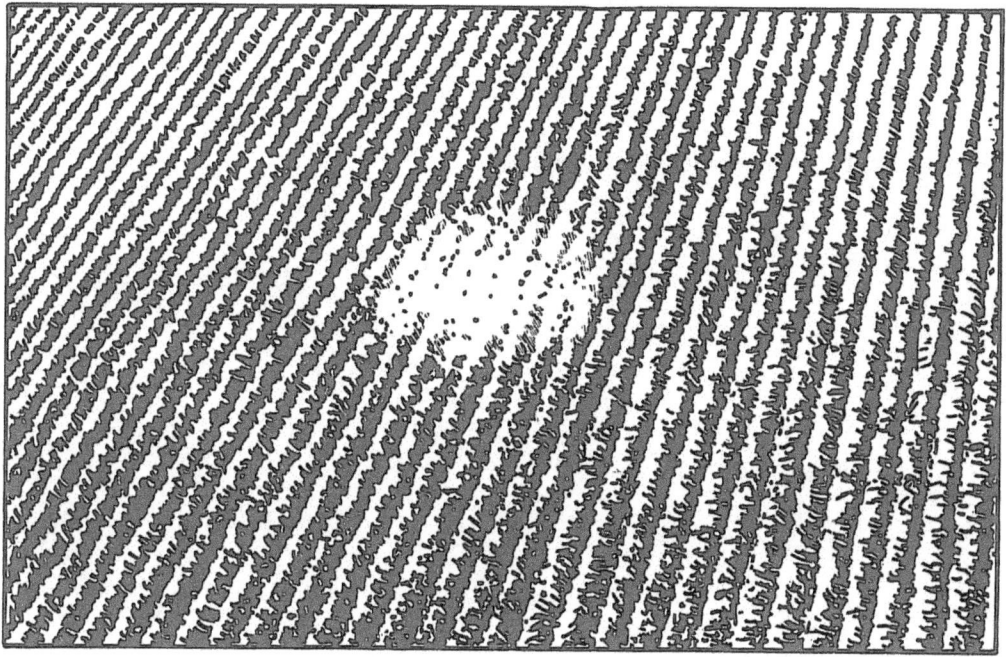

In 1969 marks left on an Iowa farmer's soybean field were reportedly made by a UFO (a lighted ship of some kind) hovering over the area. Investigators were unable to explain them.

Hypothesize as to what might have caused the scorch marks if they were not caused by a UFO.

Close Encounters of the Third Kind

You have just had a close encounter of the third kind: you have been approached by visitors from another planet and willingly have accompanied them aboard their spacecraft. You report the event to the police, but they do not believe you. Neither do your friends nor family.

List the adjectives that describe how you feel.

1.   6.

2.   7.

3.   8.

4.   9.

5.   10.

Now write an entry in your diary.
Describe how you felt before, during and after the encounter.

Dear Diary,

Alien Anthropologist

Imagine that you have met a friendly alien from a distant planet. The alien asks you to give it 20 objects that would be representative of life in your town. Assuming that neither size nor cost is an object, what would you give to the alien so that it could teach its fellow creatures about your culture?

1.
2.
3.
4.
5.
6.
7.
8.
9.
10.
11.
12.
13.
14.
15.
16.
17.
18.
19.
20.

Before the alien leaves, it asks if you would like to send a message to the inhabitants of its planet. Write your message.

_____
_____
_____
_____
_____
_____
_____
_____

© 1987 Educational Impressions, Inc.

Strange Spectator

Imagine that you are an uninvited visitor to Earth from a distant planet. You have been instructed by your superiors to keep a record of all you see. Write an account of each of these events from the point of view of an alien reporting to his/her own planet.

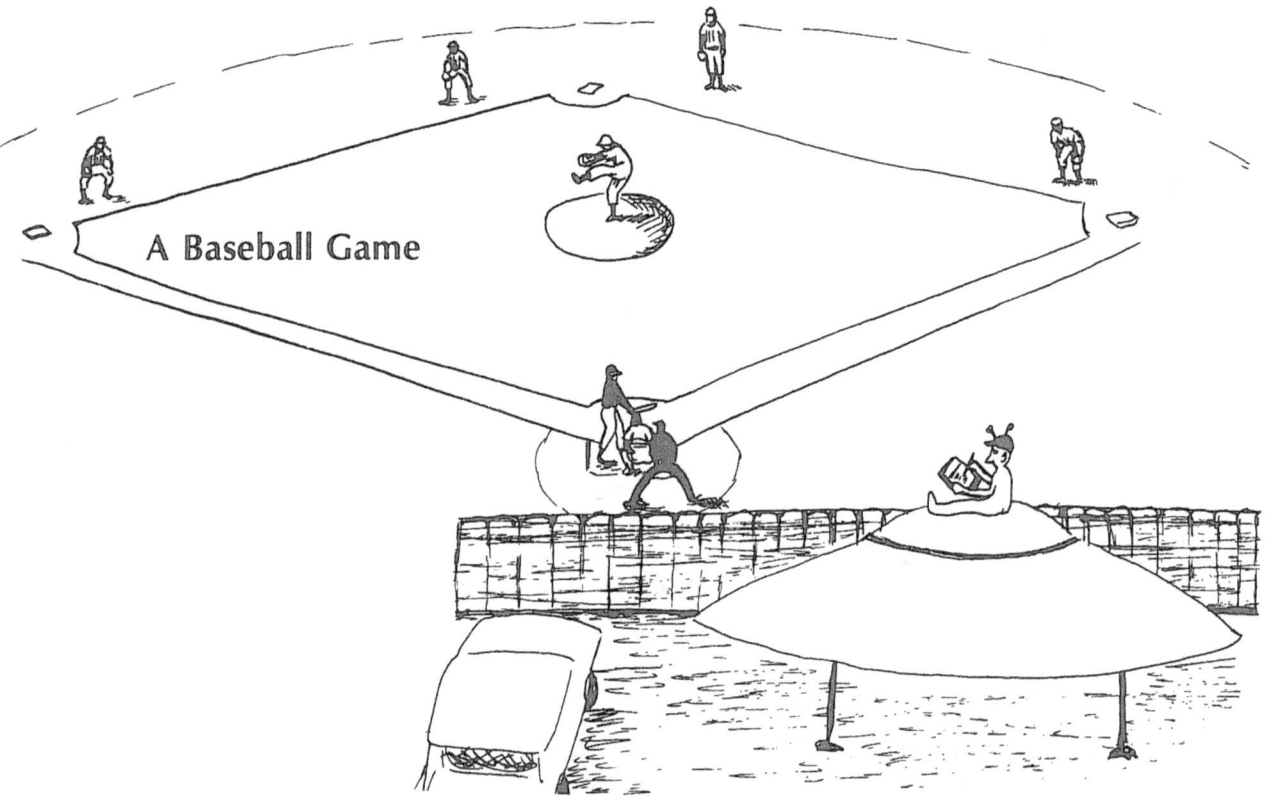

A Baseball Game

A Tennis Match

A Drive-in Movie

Thirty Tons of *What?*

In 1954 there was a wave of UFO sightings in France. Once incident involved a man who said he had seen two humanoids who apparently had arrived at the scene in a strange, long machine which had landed on the railroad tracks near his home. The man described the beings as human-like but very small; their clothing, he said, resembled a scuba diving suit. The man also reported that he had attempted to approach the machine, but as he neared it, it emitted a green light that shone upon him and paralyzed him! When the machine lifted off the ground and the beings disappeared, he was able to move again. Officials could find no footprints or other evidence that the beings had been there. Railroad officials, however, said that marks found on the wooden railroad ties in the area where the machine reportedly sat had to have been made by an object weighing at least thirty tons!

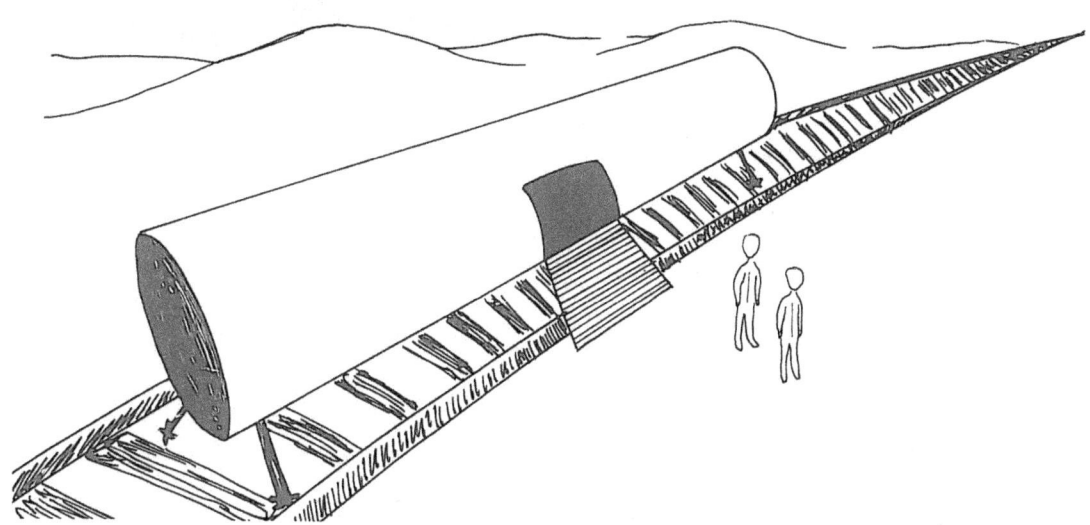

Suppose you did not believe the man's story. What could have caused the marks on the railroad tracks? Be creative and try to think of as many unusual answers as you can!

1.

2.

3.

4.

5.

6.

7.

8.

9.

10.

There's So Much to Ask!

Imagine that you have been taken aboard an alien spacecraft. The aliens are able to understand what you say and, although you don't understand how, you also understand them.

What questions do they ask you?

1.

2.

3.

4.

5.

6.

What questions do you ask them?

1.

2.

3.

4.

5.

6.

What's the Question?

These are the answers you give to your alien captors as they question you about life on your planet. Write several possible questions to which each might refer.

1. _____?
   _____?
   _____?

"They are not overly aggressive, but will fight back if provoked."

2. _____?
   _____?
   _____?

"It's a lovely place. I often go there to enjoy the peace and quiet."

3. _____?
   _____?
   _____?

"She's a very powerful individual."

4. _____?
   _____?
   _____?

"We enjoy their company, but we will never give them the right to vote."

5. _____?
   _____?
   _____?

"It's a great place to visit, but I wouldn't want to live there!"

© 1987 Educational Impressions, Inc.

What Can You Make of These?

Make pictures of objects out of the letters U-F-O.

U F O

U F O

U F O

© 1987 Educational Impressions, Inc.

UFO Sounds

In 1966 a woman in Ohio reported the sighting of a brightly lighted object hovering over the neighborhood. Two deputies were sent to investigate. When they arrived at the scene, they saw an object that grew brighter and brighter. All was quiet except for a hum. The deputies reported what they had seen and heard to police headquarters. As instructed, they followed the object when it moved. They chased it into Pennsylvania until it finally rose high into the sky and disappeared. The deputies reported the incident to Air Force officials, who dismissed it as a mirage. One deputy in particular was subjected to a great deal of ridicule by the authorities and friends alike. The movie *Close Encounters of the Third Kind* was to some extent a dramatization of his experiences.

To hum is to make or emit a continuous low droning sound like that of the speech sound "m" when prolonged. List all the things that you can think of that hum. Be creative!

Some witnesses of UFO sightings have reported that they heard a buzzing sound. List everything you can think of that buzzes!

An "Alien's" Point of View

Suppose beings from another planet landed on Earth. Describe Earth from each alien's point of view.

Alien #1: landed in Las Vegas, Nevada

Alien #2: landed in an American high school during a pep rally

Alien #3: landed in Disneyland in time for the parade

Earthly Artifacts

Suppose beings from a planet in a distant solar system landed on Earth but stayed only long enough to gather a few artifacts. From their point of view brainstorm the possible functions of those artifacts: a toothbrush, a glove, a helmet and an ironing board.

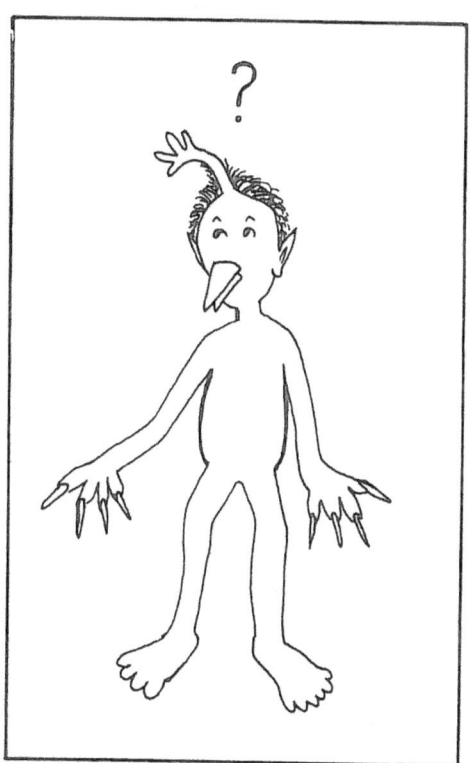

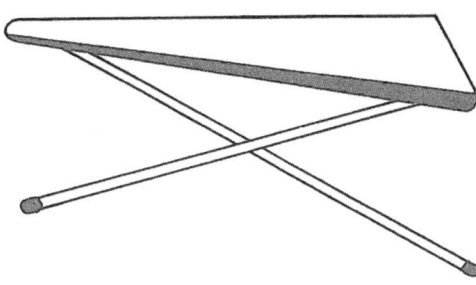

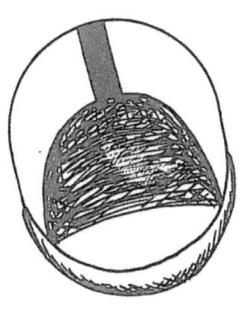

© 1987 Educational Impressions, Inc.

An Eventful Drive

On September 19, 1961, Betty and Barney Hill were driving from Montreal, Canada, to their home in Portsmouth, New Hampshire. According to their story, they saw a UFO in the form of an extremely bright light before everything went completely blank. A few hours later, when they finally became aware of where they were, they were miles from the spot where they had seen the light. Because of the nightmares and headaches that followed the experience, the Hills went to a psychiatrist who specialized in hypnosis. Separately they told of having been taken aboard the UFO and subjected to a painless but humiliating examination. They both said that they were told they would remember nothing of the occurrence. Betty also told of a star chart that she was shown which showed the home base of the beings. The two stars which she identified would not be discovered until 1969 — 2 years later!

What questions might you ask the Hills to determine if they were telling the truth?

Can you offer any explanations that could account for the story if there were really no aliens?

War of the Worlds

On October 30, 1938, Orson Wells dramatized H. G. Wells's *War of the Worlds* on his radio show. Although he announced from time to time that it was fiction, many of his panic-stricken listeners believed the broadcast of the Martian invasion of New Jersey was authentic.

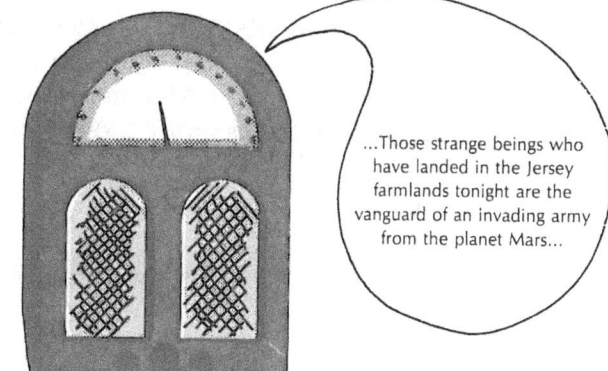

...Those strange beings who have landed in the Jersey farmlands tonight are the vanguard of an invading army from the planet Mars...

Suppose you turned on the radio and heard a credible, well-respected broadcaster announce that your community was being invaded by beings from another planet. What would you do?

_____
_____
_____
_____
_____

Assuming that the invasion was not real, describe the possible consequences of such a broadcast.

_____
_____
_____
_____
_____

© 1987 Educational Impressions, Inc.

Flying Saucers

Sometimes UFO's are referred to as flying saucers. The term was originated by Kenneth Arnold, a trained pilot, who claimed to have seen silvery, disk-shaped crafts that looked like flying saucers. He spotted them dashing over the peak of Mount Rainier in the state of Washington.

Make pictures of objects out of these "flying saucers."

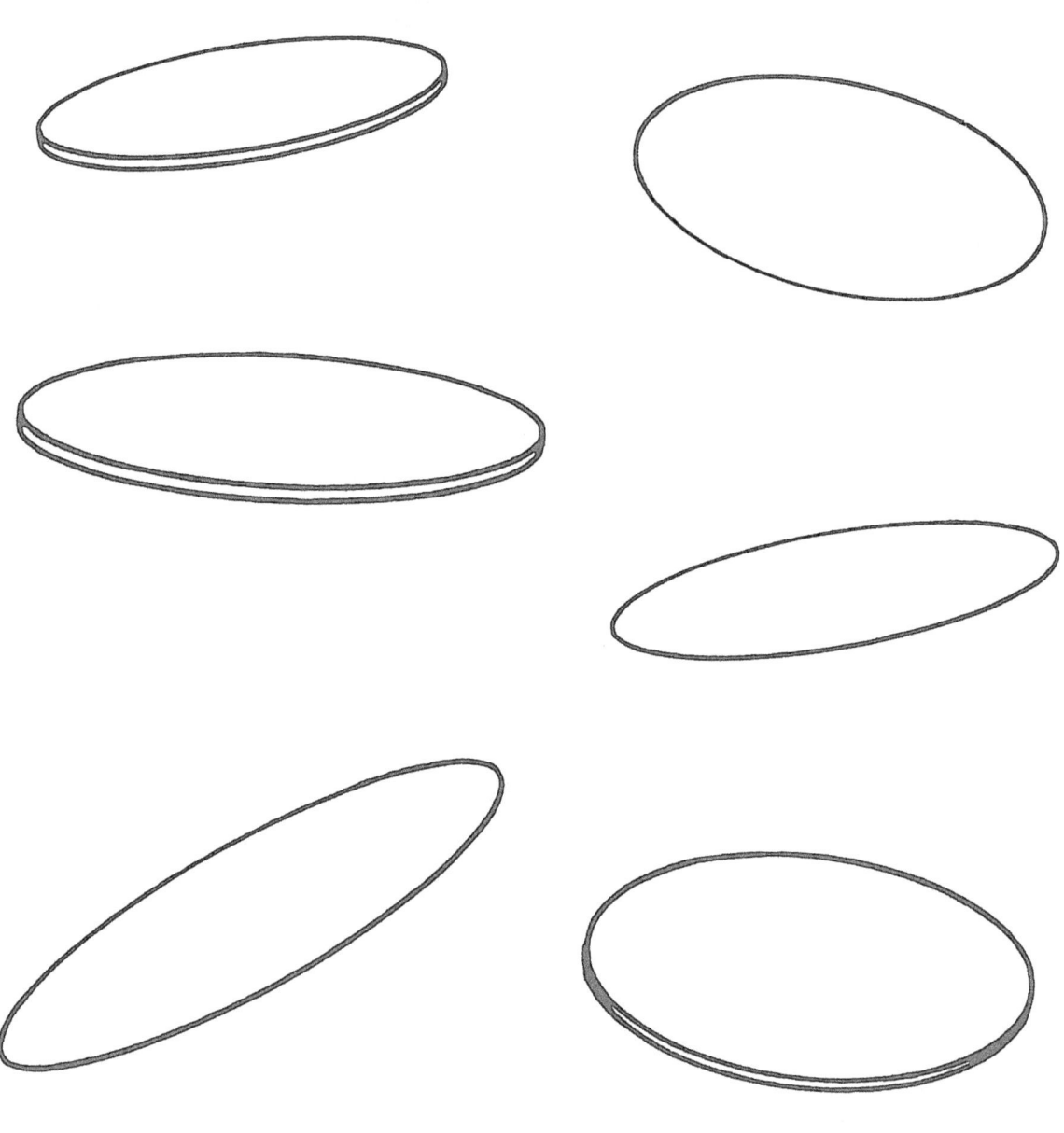

Follow-up Activities

1. Compare and contrast a yeti and a sasquatch.

2. Research and report upon the Mayas.

3. Research and report upon a mysterious place not presented in this activity book.

4. Write an original story in which the sighting of a UFO becomes exaggerated into much more.

5. We have sent unmanned space probes to study distant planets in our solar system. Write an account of a UFO sighting of these probes by a creature of one of those planets.

6. Research one of the following mysterious places: Stonehenge, Easter Island or the Pyramid at Cheops. Tell what is mysterious about it.

7. In 1968 the U.S. Air Force sponsored a study of the UFO controversy. The study was carried out under the direction of E.U. Condon, a well-known physicist. The study covered 59 sightings. Research and report on the results of the Condon Report.

8. In 1948 the U.S. Air Force began to maintain a file on UFO reports. The file was called *Project Blue Book*. Research and report on *Project Blue Book*. Evaluate its effectiveness.

9. Create your own unusual creature. Describe its physical characteristics. Also describe its social groups. Draw a picture.

© 1987 Educational Impressions, Inc.

10. Write a story about your pet yeti. What special problems do you encounter? Are there any advantages of having such a pet? What does it eat? Where do you keep it? What do you call it?

11. Create a ghost for a mystery story. Tell who the person was, how he/she died and why he/she became a ghost.

12. Suppose you met someone with psychic abilities. Make a list of questions about the future that you would like to ask the individual.

13. Write a law that would protect creatures such as Bigfoot, the yetis and the Loch Ness Monster.

14. Take a survey to find out how many people believe that UFO's may be visitors — or at least vehicles — from other planets. Analyze your findings according to age, sex, education, etc.

15. Make a diorama that shows Bigfoot, the Abominable Snowcreature or Nessie in its natural environment.

16. Some archaeologists believe that Atlantis was really a Minoan civilization. Research Solon's description of Atlantis. Then research the Minoans. Tell why some believe that there is a connection between this civilization and Atlantis. (Solon was a statesman and poet of ancient Athens.)

17. Research the voyage of Amelia Earhart. Hypothesize as to what went wrong and what happened to her.

www.ingramcontent.com/pod-product-compliance
Lightning Source LLC
Chambersburg PA
CBHW081349040426
42450CB00015B/3362